DANCES WITH DESTINY:

UNFORGETTABLE PAS DE DEUX

BY

CLAIRE MARKETTE

Dances with Destiny: Unforgettable Pas de Deux: Published by Claire Markette

First Edition: 2015

Cover Art by: [Iapencia]/Fotolia

Editing by: Nikki Busch

ISBN-13 978-0692517055
ISBN-10 0692517057

Contents

ENSEMBLES

PARTNERING

The author thanks all her former dancing partners for helping to pave a path to her destiny through their love and inspiration.

Dance 1

If Brothers Had Been Sisters

I always had a warm, close relationship with my three brothers, even though two of them were quite a bit older. When I was very young, they would gently tease me or tussle with me until my mother called for them to stop so I wouldn't "become a tomboy." As I recall, they were always there to comfort and protect, except for the younger one, whom I protected, being the older sister.

I grew up surrounded by masculinity, and more often than not, listened to dinner table conversation about carburetors, RBIs, and field goals rather than fashions or hairstyles. My mother and I were hopelessly outnumbered.

The alien world of boys' bedrooms, painted in shades of blue or brown, greeted the curious female visitor with lots of strength and action and the smell of model glue and sweaty socks. I remember raising myself up on shiny patent leather shoes to peek at the top of a maple dresser that had been converted to the Pacific Ocean or a World War II airfield. Patriotic grey-blue plastic models of planes, aircraft carriers, and battleships proudly awaited their creator who was at school. The intricate radar stations swiveled and turrets turned, and the delicate wires with multicolored flags and insignias connected the masts and decorated imposing vessels, representing real ships that sailed the seas and fought for liberty. Tiny pink fingers were tempted to slowly swirl propellers, and the little rubber wheels glided so smoothly across the wooden runway!

My dolls were lifelike—they made noises and had pretty names and could be cuddled. Planes and ships only had black numbers and letters on the sides but held some sort of strange tough power I couldn't quite comprehend. Other bedroom treasures included stacks of comic books about spaceships and Martians, parts of Boy Scout uniforms, and a globe of the world that I found fascinating and loved to spin to find pink France or orange Spain.

As my brothers grew older, the rooms changed, reflecting their new pursuits: stacks of 45 RPM records replaced *Superman* comics; pigskin footballs and tan baseball gloves occupied a vacant chair; varsity letters and high school pennants adorned the walls; and the aircraft carrier and battleships now shared the high seas with picture frames of prom snapshots, torn movie ticket stubs, and drama programs.

But what if these three musketeers had been gentle female creatures, vying for my father's attention? Three sisters instead of three brothers? My world would have been quite different. Instead of dark blue and brown, bedroom walls would have probably been pink or lavender, awash in nylon and lace, and families of dolls and plush animals might have populated dainty white shelves. Whiffs of perfume and bubble bath would have replaced the odor of sweat and model glue.

Conversations would have been hushed whispers or excited shrieks about prom dresses, hair styles, or lipstick shades. Dressers might hold musical jewelry boxes with twirling ballerinas, or makeup kits, and the floor would be littered with issues of *Teen* or *Glamour* magazines instead of comic books. My father would have been outnumbered, not daring to display his masculine supremacy against a chorus of sopranos sweetly pleading to purchase just one more crinoline.

Suddenly, the thought of these three temptresses struck jealousy and fear into my heart! Would they have wanted to borrow my clothes? No, I am sure their ages would have rendered sizes incompatible. But what about size-less items like scarves and bracelets? Two older sisters! Then most of my clothes might have been handed down from sister to sister. Being the third girl would have made this a distinct possibility. Would I have had to share my bedroom with one of these vixens? What I might have gained in experience, sisterly wisdom, and secret sharing I would have lost in privacy and exclusive pampering, and the special fatherly affection I received for being the only female sibling would have been divided four ways.

If sisters meant "borrowing" my makeup, fighting for first rights to the bathroom, or snooping in my diaries, I'd gladly forego the pleasure and put up with batting practice in the hallway and sweaty gym socks on the stairs. I'm glad the fates decided to bless my parents with only one pink bundle of bliss instead of four. I'll take brothers any day!

Dance 2

High School Dream

The heavy front door slammed behind me as I entered the large foyer, and the brash sound of chain links swinging against the wide metal door handle told me I was back at the high school where I had spent four long years in an earlier life.

I passed rows of sports trophy cabinets, and the beige painted walls were full of engraved plaques, commemorating students and teachers who had long since vanished. I looked down at the penny loafers I was wearing and checked the year of the shiny coin I must have placed between the leather flaps—1966.

Just ahead of me, in front of the French doors leading to the courtyard stood a naked Christmas tree, waiting to be trimmed.

The hollow echo of my footsteps reverberated in the empty hallway as I hurried past the auditorium. Through the gap in the double doors, I could see several students on stage, apparently rehearsing for a holiday play. I stopped and gently pulled on the door to open it just a crack so I could eavesdrop.

"Stage left you dimwit!" shouted the male. It was Rob Bennett, voted most courteous in the class yearbook. I remembered that he had captured the lead in the annual spring production with his silvery smooth voice and good looks. He snarled and snapped at the girl while he paced nervously back and forth on the stage.

I heard his co-star suddenly yell, "One more outburst from you and I quit!" It was the lovely Jennifer Malone, Miss Popularity. Her hourglass figure and long blonde hair helped her achieve prom queen status, but as I examined her from a fresh perspective, I noticed a shrill, unpleasant voice and an ever so slight limp. Was this the perfect woman I wished I could have been like and had tried to emulate? My ears stung when I heard the profanity emerge from her pouty red lips, and I closed the door and moved on.

I wondered where everyone else was and climbed the metal stairway to the second floor. Peering into the door of room 209, I spotted my best friend listening intently to Mrs. Frederickson, the English teacher. She was droning on about Shakespeare in her boring monotone voice and I could see that the class was having a hard time concentrating. Why did I ever think she was a "good" teacher? I could see Susan Swenson furtively gazing into her compact mirror and wetting her lips, not paying any attention to the teacher's words of wisdom. Since she had been voted the best dressed in our class, I took note of what she was wearing: a beige corduroy jumper trimmed in brown wooden buttons over a white Peter Pan-collared blouse and a gold charm bracelet on each wrist. Compared to anyone else's clothes, hers were a cut above, but she was certainly no fashion plate! I guess it helped to have a father in the wholesale jewelry business and a mother who was head buyer of a chic boutique store.

Passing my history classroom, the teacher spotted me and shouted, "You're late! Where's your pass?"

I murmured something about not being able to get one and slid into the seat beside Charlie Bower, the bookworm who later became a brilliant lawyer. I focused on the blackboard and saw the word "Current Events" underlined with "Vietnam" written underneath. As I listened to Mr. Linton talk about the merits of bombing, I suddenly realized what a hawk he had been. I didn't dare raise my hand to tell him we had lost the war. I just hoped he wouldn't call on me to present my current event topic. Would he believe that the Berlin Wall had been torn down or would he send me to the principal's office for being a rude smart aleck? Then I recognized a steady, serious voice from the back of the room, as its owner raised a question. I turned to see Amy, who would become valedictorian. Tears welled in my eyes as I recalled how she was killed in a car accident one week after graduation. The bell rang and I stood up to leave. Rude students pushed past me, not bothering to be cordial. The hallway turned into a cattle stampede and the sound of banging locker doors meant lunchtime.

As I wandered along feeling deserted, I recognized myself…shy, withdrawn, somehow outside of this reality and not part of this little world of pretention and bravado. I drifted downstairs and stood for a minute in the front foyer. I felt as lonely and as unadorned as the undecorated tree. Then I suddenly remembered that I had surpassed all of this long ago. This shallow, empty world I had had to endure for four years was not as it had seemed back then. I had imagined classmates with special, polished personalities when in fact they were only people with imperfections, just like me.

Time and maturity had brought a sense of perspective to those difficult, confusing days. I hurried out the front door and breathed in the fresh air, feeling better about myself by being able to accept the past for what it was: a time to hurt, a time to learn, a time to forget.

Dance 3

Culture Shock—1970

No matter how many times I hear the song "Cecilia" by Simon and Garfunkel, I will always see a dark Swiss cellar restaurant and hear a lively group of American students singing the lyrics.

We met our French teacher for a typical Swiss dinner of melted raclette cheese and boiled fingerling potatoes, so that we might be exposed to some local culture while practicing French.

My classmates and I descended into the dimly lit "cave" and found our way to a large wooden table along one wall. Our teacher, a pale thin woman who almost never smiled, ordered dinner for us, and we began to absorb the restaurant's subtle atmosphere. As we settled back on the dark polished benches, sipping our crisp, cold white wine, the Swiss students in our group began to sing, as was their custom in less formal eating establishments. The other patrons seemed to enjoy this spirited outpouring of simple rustic melodies and joined in to sing nationally known classics about peaceful mountains and pride of homeland. The singing ceased when our dinner was delivered on small warm plates, and we tasted the soft, mild, almost-liquid cheese while the other students chatted and joked.

Suddenly, one of our foreign classmates pointed a finger at us.

"Now it is your turn. You must sing us some American songs!"

I don't remember who decided on singing "Cecilia," but it had been popular at home when we left. Perhaps someone thought we needed relief from a somewhat sterile and innocent mood.

We began singing the lyrics, laughing to ourselves while visualizing the risqué scene. We noticed the foreign students straining to catch the words and translate the strange phrases. On we sang with abandon, tapping out the rhythm on the wooden tables. We were empowered knowing something that the foreign students couldn't understand or appreciate. Oh what decadence they were missing!

Then we noticed our teacher's ashen face, a mirror of shock and disdain. Perhaps we were getting carried away—why hadn't we chosen "Bridge over Troubled Water" or "Blowing in the Wind"? Our brashness diminished somewhat, and we finished, not daring to repeat another stanza. The chatter at the other tables seemed to quiet abruptly, and we tried to make small talk. The Swiss students began to beg the teacher to translate our song since they apparently had not understood its full meaning. Her sullen reply was direct. "No. It is a very dirty song" she told them in French. "Trés sale!"

They looked at us incredulously and we were unable to vent our denials in front of this conservative bastion of propriety. The singing had ceased for the evening. The waiter brought us tiny cordial glasses of strong kirshwasser to sip.

"Good for the digestion," the teacher remarked. "Dip a sugar cube into it."

I lowered the cube gently over the top of my glass, but suddenly lost my grip, and the cube floated on top, slowly descending and melting into the pure, after-dinner liqueur and into oblivion.

I turned to her sheepishly and asked, "Was that a terrible faux pas?"

She nodded affirmatively, as if delighted that by chance, circumstance had punished the sinful.

The waiter delivered the bill. We got up to leave, humming our song in low tones, glad to be Americans in this land of uptight rigidity and rule-bound limitations, where women were still not allowed to vote!

Dance 4

Kurt

I was a fragile and innocent college sophomore, yearning to meet someone exciting at long last, after spending too many years being disappointed. I had even become cynical, trying to insulate myself against hurt. Popular song lyrics about being a rock and an island persuaded me to try and protect myself.

"If you're a freshman and a girl, you know Kurt Von Ronnen," a knowledgeable junior once told me, but I chose to disregard this friendly bit of information.

Something electric was in the air that Friday night, as I walked in to my girlfriend's second floor apartment to attend a surprise birthday party for a mutual friend from high school. I wore a conservative green linen dress, and my dark, shoulder-length hair brushed its rolled collar.

As I struggled with a stubborn soda cap, a skinny blond pre-med student who lived upstairs came to my rescue. He had just walked in and I was instantly attracted to him. His deep green eyes penetrated mine with sincerity, and mine sparkled back at the thought of romance. So this was the Kurt whose reputation was so renowned!

He spoke with a polished German accent which I adored, and his wire-rimmed glasses seemed to complete the portrait of a soft-spoken, continental intellectual. The attentiveness he showed me was even more attractive than his voice, and I longed to know this stranger. Kurt drank the tea I offered him, even though he said he didn't like all the sugar I had added. We sat in the kitchen and listened to the new Beatles album, and he played with a blue-and-green papier-mâché parrot hanging across the doorway between the kitchen and living room.

To experience a crush is to live in a whirlwind; everything around you moves quickly and rushes by without your notice. You are focused on another person and nothing else matters. When you think you're in love, you write everything down that the special one says, to be able to understand the spoken words when you are finally alone, because your ear doesn't comprehend when your mind is clouded with such a vision. You write poetry about him and dream about him, and practice scribbling "Mrs." in front of his first and last name, endlessly across a blank page. You count the days until you will meet him on his way to his second period Bacteriology lecture on Thursdays, making sure to wear your best sweater and jeans and putting on just enough perfume for him to notice. If you happen to accidentally bump into him in the cafeteria, your whole day is pink and warm and everyone is your friend.

"He's in the lab looking through a microscope, dressed in a suit waiting to be called for his yearbook picture," reported a friendly spy. I hoped to meet Kurt around every corner. Would he show up at the dinner dance I had paid twenty dollars to attend in hopes of getting the chance to be with him again? As soon as I saw him board the bus I knew the night held promise.

The evening grew more enchanting when he sat down next to me at our table after dinner and invited me to dance. We talked about Kafka and I tasted his martini. He told me the paella he had ordered for his meal was "an abortion" and said something about burning the candle at three ends and probably dying by the time he was thirty. We walked together to the bus under the winter stars, and he sat with me and took my hand in his, telling me it was cold. "Cold hands, warm heart," he whispered in my ear. I was in heaven, and I wished the night would never end. But it did.

Kurt filled my diaries and invaded my dreams until we actually planned a date. My heart pounded as we drove away from my house and I tried to remember the cute phrases I had memorized to use with him.

We parked at the drive-in movie but spent the evening talking and kissing, which was fine with me. I didn't care for westerns and wanted to learn all about his life. As we talked, I slowly realized that I didn't know him at all. His world was not mine, and I found him wise beyond his years and jaded beyond hope. He felt inferior to an older sibling and said that if he had to lose one faculty he would choose his sight over all the others. He said he thought I was a romantic and that he didn't want to hurt me. Kurt was sure he could bounce back but he wasn't sure about me.

He lit a cigarette, and we conversed endlessly about relationships and feelings. He said he thought I could be very passionate and took on a superior tone when he said he pitied me for being so protected and naïve. I began to feel uneasy.

We walked to my front step and he told me not to look down, but always up. He mentioned something about wanting to see me again, and not thinking, I murmured "Oh, I don't know." Then he turned and was gone.

And suddenly I DID know. I DID want to see him again! Now came the longing, the regret, the hopeful reunion, and the missed opportunities. Time raced on, while I lingered in the abyss of confusion and indecision, not knowing how to begin again with him, uncertain of his feelings, and unsure of what to say or when to say it. I was lost, losing all I had gained, yearning to get it back, but not knowing how.

I arrived early for German class, knowing that he would emerge from the same room while my class waited in the hallway to go in. The obligatory visit to the powder room across the hall assured me of looking perfect. This ritual lasted for months, but I never made much progress. Shy and afraid, I was only able to stammer hello and talk about unimportant things, until he had to rush off to his next class. He was likely mistaking anxiety for polite reserve, and probably assumed we were just good friends now.

Once, after saying good-bye to him and then learning that our class was cancelled, I raced out the door to see him walking ahead of me on the sidewalk. Should I speak to him? As he nonchalantly tossed his cigarette butt onto the pavement before him and sprinted ahead, unaware of my presence, the wind caught the burning end and it rolled back toward me. I almost picked it up to retain some part of him forever—but I didn't. Not out of shyness, but because I realized how silly and romantic the idea was, and how useless. Perhaps I was growing out of naiveté and into the world of reality at last. Perhaps I knew it was really over and that I had to go on without him. But for many years his voice lingered in my head and thoughts of what might have been tugged at my heart. I was not content because this "thing" had never really been finished. I hoped to resolve it within myself but it wouldn't go away. It just remained to cloud my thinking and invade my relationships with other men. He came to me in dreams and I wrote about him privately, hoping that one day I would meet him again and finish what we had started.

Dance 5

The Perfect Guy

Declan appeared to have what every woman wanted—an attractive appearance, a fun-loving sense of humor, a quick intelligent mind, and a sensitive and gentle side to his nature. He seemed to be an instant success at parties, and his popularity with women was renowned.

But did the reputation that followed him like a faithful little puppy actually mirror reality? Was this picture of a carefree, happy bachelor only a façade? If so, what lay behind the outward glow of this supposed man about town?

He was the middle child of an upper-middle-class family, who was sent to nursery school to learn to socialize. He endured several minor surgical operations when young and forever after became preoccupied with health concerns. After only a few dates, women would invariably be told that he was "stressed out" and consequently feeling ill; it was a good excuse for sympathy or for breaking a date.

His mother doted and worried over him. "Please don't buy a motorcycle," she pleaded. "Remember what happened to the neighbor's son!" Declan said his mother and father had a good marriage, because every Saturday evening they would go out for dinner and dancing.

He did the normal things that most teenagers do, which included playing in a band and helping to repair houses for a relative during summer breaks from college. He also had a steady girlfriend.

In college he had trouble relating to others and often spent time alone. He taught school for a while but then realized that a brighter future lay outside the classroom. Somewhere along the way, he decided that a different career might bring him more money and prestige, and he worked toward that ambitious and realistic goal. He planned out this transition and had intended to move up to more responsible positions in publishing as time went on. I wonder just when and how this change came about. When did he begin to build this mystique about himself, this aura which surrounded him? Did it coincide with growing a beard to somehow create a charade to hide behind?

Declan loved to enjoy himself, not by surrounding himself with material possessions, but by using people and circumstances to get his own way. He had a marvelous knack for manipulating women (had he practiced on his mother?) and playing them against each other. He enjoyed making them mad so he might get the chance to be reprimanded. Was this yearning for discipline a need that was never fulfilled in youth?

Here was a man who "needed his space" as the saying goes. His haphazard dating patterns kept him constantly moving, never having to be pinned down, never being able to make a commitment, except for a superficial kind of temporary friendship. This loner became more and more distant and empty and so did his relationships with others. He once said that all romantic encounters become less intense over time and that nothing remains as wonderful as it first seems. He found that a real enigma—something he couldn't seem to control and something about which he felt sad and helpless. Or was he somehow *making* the relationship less because he did not want to commit himself to one person? Had he been so deeply hurt that he couldn't give? Or didn't he want to give?

Maybe Declan just never discovered the key to building a true relationship and never understood how to love. Late at night, he admitted that the distance he put between himself and his partners might be his tragic flaw. If he couldn't change, he was doomed to playing games with women until the smart ones figured out how to hurt him back, by breaking a New Year's Eve date too late for him to find someone else.

This "perfect" guy was NOT really so perfect after all.

Dance 6

A Bridge to the Future

Colin was my bridge, transporting me from those, sad, unhappy days of marital separation and divorce into a world of excitement and laughter. Whenever he phoned, his deep seductive but playful voice would instantly push those hopeless thoughts from my worried mind. His positive, carefree attitude helped to dull the pain that seemed to follow me everywhere, and his sense of humor cut through that invisible cloud of depression into which I was enveloped, where everything and everyone seemed unreal and unapproachable. His light, blue-grey eyes sparkled behind a pair of silver-rimmed, square-cut glasses. His straight, raven-black hair, streaked with strands of grey, fell just slightly across his rather wide forehead, and the well-groomed mustache half-framed a broad and friendly smile.

Colin's tall, thin body sported lovely broad shoulders that looked more magnificent in his navy-blue blazer and made his slim

28

waist appear even trimmer. As he sauntered down the hallway, his jaunty, carefree swagger displayed assertive self-assurance and serene composure. As far as I could see, nothing ever bothered this bon vivant. I welcomed someone who enjoyed life as much as he must and longed to know more about him.

Those strong muscular arms and long fingers seemed to attract me like magnets, drawing me toward him for protection. One short visit from him could heighten my awareness to a new level with just a few light-hearted phrases and some sips of wine. It was as if he had suddenly turned darkness into daylight simply by being near. He could leave me feeling wonderful, but at the same time confused.

As I continued to study this paragon of strength, he slowly began to reveal his weaknesses to me. "Don't trust me" he would warn. Little by little, the things he said or did disclosed his insecurity. I began to be doubtful and wary of the things Colin sometimes told me. He was a real paradox. His gentle, caring attitude and generous response to my emotional needs at a time when I very much needed someone to listen, conflicted with this selfish, often cryptic personality. He broke more than one date and liked to mention other female "friends" he had dated. Did he think that making me jealous would enhance our relationship as it seemed to do for him? Or was he just putting distance between us in a casual way? Everywhere I turned there were twists. "I like someone to tell me no meaning yes," he would say. "When you are mad, you are beautiful," he would declare.

But the roles shifted. Now I was the one he was calling strong. I was the one to be consulted about life's little crises. Colin swiftly guided me into a world I never had the opportunity to experience, and perhaps made me even stronger, enduring the never-ending games and nuances of our relationship. I have been filled with the greatest heights of passion and the darkest depths of despair because of him. Yet he brought such joy into my life and helped me to realize some truths that I needed to uncover, to feel fulfilled as a woman of the eighties, and to cross that bridge to the future.

Dance 7

That Perfect Afternoon

My diary is full of you, from the first time I felt something special for you. You said I could put that special day in my diary...well I did just as you thought I would. I don't write there much anymore. I have little to write about that excites me. I miss your hang-up phone calls, and the ones I get now are probably not from you. I miss the sound of your voice, your questions and compliments, your strong hands, and your warm embrace. I often wonder what you did on your birthday or on New Year's Eve, when I silently wish good things for you as I sip my champagne at midnight.

Do you remember our first drive, when all we had were questions for each other? Your tense arm on the steering wheel trying to be a barrier to the feelings I expressed? The way you asked directions when you were lost? I hardly knew you and yet I trusted you. There was something honest in the way you did things and said things. Do you remember our picnic in the rain listening to Tangerine Dream? You tried to ask me so many things that I didn't know how to or want to explain. You searched for a hidden spot, while we walked in the humid summer heat, not wanting to let this chance get away. You tore off your cap and threw it on the grass. Turning my face slowly toward yours with your large warm hand, you pressed your wet lips against mine. Your kiss was abrupt but full of passion. Then you took me in your arms. I never knew such joy!

Our bridle path is still there. It is decked out in all its green summer lushness waiting for us to come again and feel the hot sun on our backs and the cool damp grass under our bodies. The sun was hot this time and it felt good to wander under the shade trees, carefully avoiding the tree roots that were surely in our path that day, which I never noticed. I think I found that perfect spot off the path where we once shared our love and tenderly caressed each other, the soft drops of rain lightly falling from tree branches to bless us. When I came to the clearing where you tilted my head to yours and kissed me, I stopped and closed my eyes, trying to remember how it felt.

Ten years have not dimmed the elation I felt when you lifted me up to the sky or when you took my hand and swiftly led me into the inner path to our hidden lair. After we finished, you asked me how it was, and taken by surprise at your question, I murmured a weak "Okay." When you replied "just okay?" I saw your disappointment and threw my arms around you. You seemed so pleased and yet a bit overwhelmed and unsure.

"You have an inferiority complex a mile wide," I told you as we walked back to the car, and you said in a low voice, "I know." Do you remember reaching up to a low-hanging branch full of moisture, beginning to shake it above me while I laughed and dared you not to? The memory of your boyish charm still touches me. Are you still the same now? Can your bright blue, sparkling eyes still send your undivided attention to the woman you are trying to woo?

As I walked away from our special spot today, I spied two small wild daisies and picked them. Perhaps they were waiting for us to be together again.

The rose garden is still there but different now. The gazebo is gone and there are new benches. I stopped at the pink-tinged-blossomed bush called Kiev Beauty and smiled. Perhaps it is ours.

Was it there that day? I don't remember. Did you know I came back exactly one year from our date and placed two roses joined on one stem in the spot where we made love? Why did I do that? I often drive through the park and think of you, without making time to stop and wander down that lane. Do you ever stop to think of that tryst and how we might have changed the future that day if only we had had the courage?

That phone call the following week at the exact time and day of our meeting told me it was you. You did remember! You did want to be with me again! But how were we to make it happen? There were too many obstacles. Or perhaps I lacked the courage. I wonder if you ever went back to revisit our past, or think about that perfect afternoon so long ago. I wonder. I think I shall always wonder.

Dance 8

Dinner for Two

Moments after I arrived at the small hotel in Nîmes, France, dusk began to descend and transform day into evening. The French call this time the *blue hour*, when the deepening sky wraps itself slowly in an azure cloak, just before daylight melts into nocturnal darkness and adorns the heavens with dazzling, diamond-like stars. The light grew dimmer, and there was only a slight hint of a breeze when I opened the wooden window shutters of my little third-floor room. As I gazed out the window, quiet hung like a heavy tapestry over the ancient city and a lulling sense of tranquility seemed to pervade the air. Below and to the right of the room was an older wing of the hotel, which housed the large shower room. I could see right through to the tiled interior by the small window above the bathtub.

In front of me, rows of overlapping red-orange roof tiles formed a beautiful mosaic carpet underneath the darkening sky. Here and there modernity triumphed with TV antennas and a few white, round satellite dishes. Beyond the houses a church steeple slumbered under the grey-blue sky and pointed its cross upward and inward toward the immense defenseless heavens.

Below me to my left, a lovely stone house stole the last sunbeams from the clouds. A long empty wooden table stood on the patio awaiting some life from within. A small round metal table near the door of the large house held a bouquet of wildflowers with several daisy petals lying on the table's surface.

Suddenly, as I was enjoying the calm, hanging my hastily washed laundry on a clothesline I had strung across the window, someone broke the silence by opening the heavy wooden door leading to the patio of the house below. A young woman, her hands clutching plates and napkins, deftly decorated the empty table in preparation for dinner. She quickly disappeared into the house and I looked down over the neatly laid-out place settings for two. Were they lovers? Girlfriends? Husband and wife? I began to weave possible scenarios as I arranged my clothes on the small plastic line.

The girl emerged again and I suddenly smelled something delicious drifting upward toward my lonely room. A large plate of fish was placed in the center of the table and several dishes were put alongside it. The glasses were filled with white wine and the green bottle was placed on a white linen napkin.

Soon an old grey-haired woman in a black dress came slowly out of the house carrying a water pitcher. The young woman rushed to take the pitcher out of her hands and helped her to a chair. The old woman bent over her plate and began to eat very slowly. The smell of fine French food continued to drift upward and I longed to join them.

I could hear clinks of glasses and taps of utensils mingled with unintelligible conversation, and I turned away from the open window, not wanting to intrude on their meal. They were totally unaware that their dinner for two was being observed. I felt like a silent cat in a tree watching its prey. I drank my tea and wrote some postcards.

When I returned to the open window, the old woman had gone inside the house, and the girl was clearing the table. When she had carried the plate of leftover fish into the house, I gazed down at the half-empty table. No scraps for me, who had travelled all day by train and had missed dinner? At least I had shared someone's dinnertime, I thought. I began to imagine what their lives were like. Did the girl visit her grandmother every week for dinner? Or did she live with the old woman? Or was this her mother, wearing black since she was a widow? Or was this her husband's mother who lived with them? I continued to invent intricate stories about these two strangers who had dined below me, on the patio of an old French house, under an orange roof in the ancient city of Nîmes.

The plates and glasses stood forlornly on the table, waiting to be fetched. The girl came back, removed the remaining dinnerware, and closed the huge door behind her. The clank of the heavy door handle broke the silence, shutting me out of their world.

Everything was quiet. The lights in the town were beginning to glow and the old stone house was peaceful. Only the flowers remained, undisturbed. Who had picked them? I moved away from the window, wondering about the lady and the girl.

Dance 9

Mendocino

We turned off the main highway at dusk hoping to find a room for the night. The dim lights of the tiny California seaside village beckoned to us, and as we turned down Main Street they grew brighter. As we passed the church and post office, we were suddenly filled with an overwhelming sense of serenity. This little corner of our globe seemed "other worldly"…an oasis of calm. We found ourselves in the midst of charming Victorian houses, delightful curio shops, and tasteful art galleries. We passed a sign for a Bed and Breakfast and decided to stop and ask if there was a vacancy for the night.

When I returned with the key, the summer mist had become thicker, wrapping us in its warm, protective covering. We found the garden and followed the flagstone path to the private cottage behind the main house.

I slowly opened the delicate French doors. Inside, white moonlight streamed down from the skylight directly above the bed, bathing the room with a bright, warm glow. A wicker basket of soft, fluffy white towels and herbal soaps sat on a huge mahogany desk, and the Franklin stove, a sentinel ready to warm and comfort the weary, stood beside the cherry four-poster bed, which was draped in a royal-blue Laura Ashley paisley-print comforter. Mounds of pillows reposed in front of the headboard, and deep-piled, cream-colored rugs covered the white ceramic tiled floors.

We left this haven in search of dinner. The streets were quiet and the old-fashioned lamps lit our way back to Main Street. The shops were all closed but the windows invited one to pause. The church bells chimed nine times as we climbed the stairs of a restaurant overlooking the ocean. I thought life was mellow here, and it seemed as if this tiny hamlet had miraculously escaped the stress and strains of modern life.

On our walk back to the cottage, we passed beautiful gabled houses with little attic balconies framed with latticed woodwork. Behind a long white picket fence, sweet-smelling gardenia bushes and trellises of pink climbing roses nestled against clapboard.

Dim light appeared through delicate lace curtains, which no doubt hid lovely treasures within.

We turned another corner and walked down to see the beach. Tiny, docile white-edged waves tamely lapped at the brown muddy shore in the rocky alcove. A pale misty fog hung over the little town, shrouding it in peace and tucking it in for the night.

Walking back past the fancy hotel on our way to the cottage, I noticed a strange-looking man in tattered clothing trying to follow one of the guests into the hotel. He abruptly turned away and began to systematically empty the trash can that was on the curb. My illusions were shattered. Here in this tranquil setting, the harsh realities of life coexisted with gentility. Even this lovely remote village had not been spared. I was disappointed and saddened to realize this perfect spot was less than I had imagined.

As we drove away the next morning, I could see red brick chimneys quietly puffing grey wisps of hickory-scented smoke up into the clear blue sky above the picturesque houses. I wondered about the people living within those walls. Do they know that the world outside their door is not perfect? And if they know, do they care?

41

Dance 10

The Gift

Antoinette heard the clock chime and looked up from her knitting. Her dark weary eyes looked across to the mantel above the fireplace and wandered from left to right, noting each item: her faded wedding portrait, the silver candleholder, the ticking timepiece, her daughter's bronzed baby shoes, and finally her favorite sculpted curio. This special gift was the only memento she had left of Michel. As her tired eyes settled on this last object, she threw her head back and slowly began to rock in the old oak chair. Gently she took out her hairpins one by one and let her long, silky auburn tresses cascade down her calico-covered back. She closed her tear-filled eyes.

Michel was standing before her, presenting her with a white box tied with a wide lavender ribbon. She opened the lid and carefully lifted the heavy object out of its nest and began to unwrap her birthday present. As the sheets of tissue fell away, she stared at the exquisitely carved stone, feeling its smooth, cold surface and tracing the tiny white outlines of blossoms etched onto the exterior.

A small narrow vase grew upward from the stone's center, and in front of it, sections of intricate carving framed the vessel with delicate filigree floral patterns. Below the bottom of the vase, a small cuplike trough had been molded out of the stone's base.

As Antoinette held the curio up to the light, shades of mahogany and slate mingled and caught the morning sunbeams, which sent them scurrying through the lattice-like designs, scattering little diamond-shaped sparkles onto the wall behind them.

She placed the gift on the marble table and Michel put a small cluster of tiny violets into the vase. He said the color of the stone seemed to match her hair. He told her how he had gone to Monsieur Rocard's antique shop that morning and how he had been captivated by the little present. The shopkeeper had acquired it from an old gypsy woman who brought him things from time to time. The gypsy had told Monsieur Rocard that happiness and good fortune would come to the first owner.

⁕

And then suddenly, her life with Michel was over. Antoinette remembered how she sobbed as she wrote the words her father commanded her to write in her farewell note to Michel.

"I cannot marry you. Meet me tonight so that I can explain and say good-bye."

She had looked up at the vase on the mantel, watching the violet petals silently dropping into the trough below, like her tears dripping onto the parchment beneath her quill pen.

Michel spent one last evening with her, leaving her a sweet bouquet of her favorite flowers he had bought from the gypsy, hoping that this talisman might work its charm. The strange blue wildflower in the center of the bouquet seemed lost among all the violets, but kept a forlorn vigil over them.

Antoinette kissed Michel good-bye and carried the vase upstairs to her bedroom so that she might keep some part of him close to her. She placed the flowers in the vase and watered them. She tried to close her eyes but sleep would not come. She stared through tears at the blue flower amid the purple cluster and slowly became drowsy. Her sad heart ached for Michel, and she turned away from his gift.

In the morning, she leaned over to breathe in the sweetness of the blossoms, hardly opening her eyes to the daylight. When she failed to detect that lovely, delicate odor, she quickly raised her eyelids. Every violet hung down along the side of the vase's rim, dry and lifeless. Only the blue wildflower remained upright. Antoinette gasped to see that the water from the vase had collected in the cup below. The hard green wildflower stem had dropped down out of a tiny hole in the bottom of the vase and all the water she had added the night before had dripped out, leaving the frail, helpless violets to wither and die.

Antoinette tried to grow plants in the trough but nothing would live more than a few days. She finally decided to place a small votive candle in the bottom. At night, when she would blow out the candle after reading, the smoke would spiral up through the lattice carving, splitting into three distinct sections. She gazed up at the tenuous letter "M" just before she fell asleep to dream of Michel.

Dance 11

Bedroom Secrets

The pavement slowly gave way to small broken stones covering packed earth, and we slowly plodded uphill high above the city, between stately rows of grapes planted on the hillsides above and below us. The tender clusters of tiny green fruit hung on slender stems shaded by broad leaves, their vines sometimes extending thin fingers across to the next row. Were they connecting with a cousin or sibling for a friendly handshake, or was it a romantic tryst hidden from the vintner's view? Each plant grew from a brown weathered stalk, looking as if it could barely nourish such delicate, tender offspring. Metal wire strung to posts furnished artificial support, and each plant stood erect, one behind the other, forming battalions to drink in the spring rains and summer sun. Like sentinels standing guard above the ancient town, these symbols of the fertile valley brought pride to the townsfolk who hoped to boast of a good harvest in the fall.

Steep narrow wooden stairs led upward to tool sheds or quaint little houses, and rustic benches along the route provided rest for the weary hikers. Delicate wildflowers edged the path. Some had tiny purple petals clustered around a yellow center, while others showed off their cream-colored miniature bells trimmed in orchid, which gently faded toward the bottom of the blossom.

The ribbon of light green river slowly wound its way west as it divided the city. Calm rivulets became rushing white-capped rapids, soothing the ear while they drowned out the sound of cars crossing the bridge.

The clock tower chimed the hour, releasing its orderly peals into the blue-white sky to mingle with cowbells coming from the distant hills, where farmers slowly drove tractors back and forth creating rows of sweet hay.

A Gothic church spire soared over the city and we continued our climb, nestled safely between grapevines full of promise, if nature complied to partner her protégés by offering sustenance and support.

We walked in spirals down the hill toward the houses and found the paved street once more. Returning to the house where he grew up, my husband went into the garden, while I climbed the stairs to his old bedroom. What thoughts had this young boy entertained here in this bedroom so long ago, I wondered? This poster of a famous American leader must have watched him studying for tests and dreaming of someday working in the United States. Did he imagine then that he would realize his wish? Did he dare hope that one day, his baby son would play beneath his bedroom window, and his wife would write poetry at the very desk he used so many nights?

Gazing out at the splendid mountains, I longed to know the child within the man I call husband. Perhaps his son would unlock the truths I cannot seem to uncover.

www.ingramcontent.com/pod-product-compliance
Lightning Source LLC
Chambersburg PA
CBHW071352130626
46556CB00005B/2143